Kindling for Your Next Fire

Kindling for Your Next Fire

A Collection of Thoughts and Poems

Victoria Backle

RESOURCE *Publications* · Eugene, Oregon

KINDLING FOR YOUR NEXT FIRE
A Collection of Thoughts and Poems

Resource Publications
An Imprint of Wipf and Stock Publishers
199 W. 8th Ave., Suite 3
Eugene, OR 97401

www.wipfandstock.com

PAPERBACK ISBN: 978-1-6667-4198-8
HARDCOVER ISBN: 978-1-6667-4199-5
EBOOK ISBN: 978-1-6667-4200-8

06/29/22

All images by Victoria Backle.

Contents

Acknowledgments

This book is dedicated to my family and friends.

To my mother, Elaine, who fearlessly guided me towards the light when I kept drawing the curtains. For believing in me, always, despite my many misadventures. Thank you for every lesson, every porch talk, every beach walk, and every laugh over a bottle of wine.

To Grams and Pop. Though we lost Grams a few years ago, she resonates in everything I do. Her laughter and dance could lift the spirit of everyone in the room. I always hope her memory lives on through my words, which she always believed in. Her last words to me were, "Don't forget to always be inspired". So, here's to staying inspired.

To Pop, who has always been the rock in my life. Thank you for teaching me what it means to live with integrity, honesty and hard work. Your unconditional love and wisdom have shaped the course of my life.

To my siblings, Alexandra and Maximilian, who have tirelessly supported my lofty ambitions for many years. Thank you for always showing up for me in every endeavor. Thank you for the endless laughs and stories. Thank you for being my best friends and confidantes.

To my bandmates, Sean, Nathan, Tyler and Travis, who have opened my heart and mind to every possibility. I will forever be grateful to all of you for teaching, guiding, and nurturing my creativity.

To my best friend, Eddie. Your loyalty and encouragement have guided me through the darkest times. Thank you for the unwavering belief in everything I do.

To my Dad, Petey Pop, Tim, Gabriel, Grandma Marianne, Aunts and Uncles, Cousins, Shatora and the rest of my circle. I love you all.

Introduction

Ever since I learned how to pick up a pencil, I was fascinated with the power of shaping stories through poetry. For many years, I neglected this love. Depression, drug addiction, marriage, divorce and death of loved ones, all felt like good reasons to give it up. Something always pulled me back in, though. Some relentless magnetic force shoved me into a calling that I couldn't resist. Here, in these pages, are pieces of my truest self. There are words and fears that I never thought other eyes would read. There are deep insecurities and triumphant successes.

I'm proud of this work. It spans over the course of so many different versions of myself. It's a piece of my constant duality, my reflection and my shadow, which are ever-changing orbs. Both of which I can never escape; only explore. This is my way of coping with the uncertainties of life. It is a peace offering to myself, an extended hand and a yearning for a hug after years of battling with myself. This is my first, and I desperately hope my last, white flag from the trenches. I am ready to end the war.

It's time.

Time to write. Time to make music. Time to find my inner truth and build a life around my voice. It is time to howl. It is time to unleash. So, here I am. Wild and seemingly unapologetic.

This book is a part of my unleashing.

So, whether these words kindle the fire in your soul, or you literally tear up the pages and light them on fire, I hope this proves useful to you in some way. Thank you for reading and holding space for my innermost thoughts. That alone is a gift I will always be grateful for.

You will never find me sitting with the cool kids.
I will forever be the queen of the underdogs.

Be

Reach in, give more, take less.
Love yourself;
Scream, dance, create, make love.
Allow yourself to heal.
Allow yourself to hurt.
Be more aware of the gods in you,
Be more aware of the gods in others.
Wake up from the dream you're in.
See yourself in the mirror of the world.
Let the snake at the base of your spine rise—
Kundalini.
Let the wise, wild shadow in you be free from her shackles—
Dark Kali Ma.
Be wholly you.
Be wholly aware.
Be.

View

My past does not define me,
But it shaped me.
Just as the ancient, raging waters of the Earth
Shaped our most breathtaking landscapes.
My landscapes are vast and ever-changing.
There are days when I am an ocean—
A boundless source of energy.
There are years when I am the desert—
Barren and ruthless.
But I am painted with a mesmerizing palette.
Looking inward, it's as if
I can see myself from the sky.
Gently gliding through each ridge,
Planting the soles of my feet on my cliffs.
Here, I can admire every red rock,
Every deep lagoon,
Every frosted peak.
I can sit on the edge of my past
And define it by every color in a sunrise.
I can call it "pink" and "blue".
No, my past does not define me,
But it gives me one hell of a view.

Samsara

There was a darkness over all my dreams last night.
A feverish haze that stomped out even the faintest of
beauty.
They seemed to be plagued with death and tragedy,
But in a fresh breath and a clear blue sky I faced my own mortality.
As a hand against a mirror can only touch itself
through a cold reflection,
So I did in a dream—
Touch a cold and inanimate version
Of me.
There is such darkness buried beneath my surfaces,
But every darkness exists only where there is depth.
And in that depth I learned
At the very end, I mean in that very last moment, I was finally
awakened.
Finally knowing that there is a beautiful duplicity in death;
Nothing mattered
When seconds before,
Everything mattered.
And, as if woven into the same blanket, I felt the
connective thread between everything and everyone.
As I raised my hands and closed my eyes to surrenderto death,
I knew,
I was surrendering to life.

Every drop of water,
In every sea,
Will have their chance
To be a wave upon the shore.

Trade

It's rather lonely in the middle
Being neither here nor there.
Just breathing, surviving;
Passing the time and then suddenly—
Lines and marks that didn't used to be there.
Shiny silver speckles at the roots of my hair.
Lately I am so hyper-aware
Of time.
There is a visible clock upon me.
Didn't I make a deal somewhere?
Isn't there a tonic or potion to keep my darkened eyes
appealing?
Didn't I insure this fragile case I so unwillingly reside in?
If there's some invisible law, didn't I abide it?
But oh, the clock, she is worn on us all.
I cannot look into your eyes any more than I can my own.
We are all tick ticking.
Tick ticking away.
I intend not to waste any precious moment,
Though I am getting older,
I am not too old to notice,
That I am free.
Bound within a fleshy prison,
But blessed with touch
And sound
And taste.
Such a beautiful perspective on this involuntary trade.

Sea

I stand before you
As if I've stood here with you forever
Your ebb is my ebb
Your tide is my tide
Sometimes I wish I could slip inside you
And sink to the bottom
Into the infinite darkness
Maybe one of your creatures would wrap its spongy
arms around me
Perhaps you could love me so strongly
I would crystallize into countless iridescent shells
So that I may live forever here
Drifting through your furious currents
Floating on the surface of your ancient dance
Trusting you fully to break me
Rebuild me
Devour me
Change me
You are the ultimate womb
And I am but a child
Wanting to crawl back in
To your warm, wet, and unpredictable belly.

What if I stopped believing in the rules of this dream?
What if I stopped behaving like the world is as it seems?

Dance

My location is undefinable.
My destination is unattainable.
I am designed and composed of particles that bend and fold,
But they only know how to replicate what's already shown.
They are not new, they are not old.
But watch how they dance.

I thought I had a plan.
I saw a future; not bright, but clean.
An image in my mind of beasts
With gentle hands and sharpened teeth.
But even in my most confident moments,
I had my palms and knees placed against the Earth;
Chasing stardom, but praying I would not be seen.

Now the curtains have drawn
And I stand upon an illuminated stage.
Waiting for a prophetic screech to sneak its way out
From behind my tongue.
It's not until I stand before you all that I realize I have none.
So instead, I dance.

So, what do you want from me?
What do you see?
What can I possibly give that I don't deliver dangerously?
When was the last time I cradled myself,
Like a mother to a child, and said,
"You will be okay"?
When was the last time I snatched the poison from my own lips

And prayed
And promised
To god, or the sun, or the trees, or my mom
That I would learn how to take care of myself?
When have I ever glanced in the mirror,
Un-sickened,
By the deep forest of grief that stood before me?

Should I wander in?
Should I lie on the edge and sleep?
Should I dance fearlessly into the trenches of my wounds
And paint the leaves with crimson and black?
I think I should dance.

I can be the beast that makes the ground tremble.
I can learn to balance and sway with the rhythm of my unpredict-
able tides,
And perhaps,
I can dance straight into the abyss.

There is so much to learn from winter trees.
Sleepy and weathered,
Sinking inward to reflect on the memories of summer.

Monster

Beneath the starry sky I wait in vain
This is where I'll keep your secrets
This is where I'll hold your pain.
Drenched in your lovely
All battered and stained
Your hands, how they hold me
Your hands, how they break.
Let's walk together through the flames
So you can cast your weary spells on me.
Here, take my willing bones—
Your foolish little monster, I will be.

Silence

Oh, sweet Silence
We are dear and long-time friends.
She holds me when I have no others
She has space for my fear and dread
She does not visit so often,
It's so loud wherever I go
Whether I am in a crowded room
Or lying in bed alone—
It is just so rarely Silence and I.
She is my lovely maiden
Always ready when I call
My Lilith, my Silence.
If her form was in the likeness of mine
I would kiss her speechless mouth
I would worship her
With wordless hymns
Silence, my soul mate,
My far too distant lover.
I know when I have you,
I don't appreciate you enough.
Is that why you hide these days?
Have you found someone else within the static?
I know I must learn to share you
I know I must savor every divine moment with you
Stay for coffee
Stay for dinner
Come to work with me
Lie with me so I can finally sleep
But you are free and promiscuous,
Always gone by morning.

The only thing worse
Than having no control
Is doing the wrong thing
With the control you had.

I wish you knew I was born to hold you—
To wash away the pain you feel.
I wish you knew you're in my dreams often—
Too often you're in my dreams often.
I remember wishing I was God,
So I could cleanse you,
And make it like it never happened.

Your sleepy soul is somewhere in the Universe,
And all I want is one suspended moment
Where our seconds can converge.

Mine

My anxiety means wanting to be touched, but not wanting to get close.

It's needing to feel wanted in order to feel self-worth.

It's staring at myself in the mirror and hating the reflection.

No, loving the reflection.

No, hating the reflection.

It's wanting to scream in a crowded room, but not wanting to open my mouth.

It's wanting to be the life of the party, but powerless over my fear of interaction.

It's wanting to feel love, but not knowing how to take it when it's offered.

My anxiety is lying awake in bed, paralyzed by week old conversations.

It's sleepless nights, tired days, and months mulling over who I was, who I am, who I will become.

My anxiety is mine.

And it's real.

The Wildest Place on Earth

I am incomplete.
If I ever was somebody,
Today is not the day.
Undersold and overlooked
Behind closed doors and lost in the crowd.
I am a ghost
A shell of something that "could be".
A flower scared to see the sun,
Afraid to meet my maker,
Petrified of center stage.
I am screaming and pounding my head,
My aching head
Can anyone hear me?
Can anybody see—
This battle playing on the big screen
This war I've waged in me?
I am so blinded by some strange light I used to know.
Some memory.
Who do we become?
Evolution seems so bleak.
Why change? Why question? Why seek?
I am alone here.
My mind is my escape.
I can see the people staring,
But I pretend I'm not awake.
I am away,
Checked out, I've escaped.
I am in the wildest place on Earth.

I call down to the great escape—
I can trick my mind,
But I cannot trick fate,
The river runs deep,
Sweeps me away
I'm going to ride these waves one day.

Salvation

One day I might just run away and head for the mountains.
I'll change my name
I'll cut my hair
I'll sail away.
After I come to terms with my own salvation.

I find comfort in hopeless adoration.
We'll run away
We'll make the time
We'll be the future.
After I come to terms with my own salvation.

Let me tie your untethered soul
Let me in where the light won't go.

Blue Whale

Why does her child scream
Like ravens in the night?
Mother, be good,
The restless are wandering
Searching for signs of life.
Father, be quiet,
Mother is sleeping—
She is a bluish kind of pale.
Father, be gentle,
Mother is swimming—
She is chasing the blue whale.
Did she slip deception in your wine?
A funnel of venom down your throat.
Did she feed you delicious lies?
So she could live, oh, mighty host.
You refused to swallow—
Was it cold and stale?
Were you simply afraid
To eat the blue whale?

Belief

On the cornerstone of a violent storm,
Sand in eyes and garments torn,
Time is neither future nor past—
This sea of wreckage is deep and vast.

Dance with us beneath your moon
Where the beasts will be arriving soon
Where the demons come to laugh and play
Where our skin can touch, burn, and fray . . .

Where we have gods, goddesses and ancient whores
Where you can fill my vessel and make it yours—
Here lies golden calves and jeweled elephants,
White doves and an olive branch.

We can cheers to all the prophets who came and went,
To all the christs that god has sent,
To the buddhas and to the priests
To all the oceans and to the trees
For all of this makes us unique—
Belief.

Now

Life is the grand rhythm.
It is the ultimate song.
It is an artist painting a self-portrait,
Burning it,
Starting over;
Only to experience the process.
A woven tapestry
Weaving itself with light
And all the space in between.
I am standing in the warmth of a star
And I call it "day"
I am inhaling life
And I call it "air".
I am, myself, a drop of paint amidst this canvas.
Not independent, nor a focal point,
But a part of a larger whole
And I call it "now".

Let's Take a Break for a Second

You can never really prepare yourself for the loss of something, no matter how much you think you've grieved before it's actually gone. So much loss this year. I feel jaded and genuinely unattached. I am a wayward boat on the sea. Anchor's up. Destination-less. For the first time ever, I am allowing the tides to take me. I am relinquishing control.

This life is not just mine. It affects everyone I touch. Everyone I hurt. Everyone I love. Everyone I abandon. Sometimes I just want to observe it all from the sidelines, but I must be held accountable. I'm aware of how high the stakes are. I bear direct witness to every flinch and heartbreak I've ever caused. I am still present for every desperately longing gaze. I maintain a stoic bitterness towards my past, but I am apologetic for all my shortcomings. I am excited for every upcoming bump and bruise. I ride on the back of my bucking horse. I seize her coarse and uncertain head. I run my fingers through her mane. I lift up my feet and ride into the desert sunset. Nothing but dust and irreconcilable hurt behind us. Red rocks to wall us in at every turn.

Maybe I *am* lost, I'll wonder, but when my toes hit the scorched and jagged rock beneath us and my skin swelters in the hellish heat; I will know I'm exactly where I'm supposed to be. There are no mirrors here. There is no place to tidy my hair or cuff my sleeves. There is no TV lying in an ancient crater waiting for me to distract and deflect. I am here. With every version of myself. And trust me, that's enough to keep the conversation flowing. I am here. With every good and bad deed. With every needling prick of regret. I am here. With every naïve hope and dream that didn't come to fruition. I am here. With a blankness.

This horse has always been my horse. She is my majestic stallion. She has carried me from chapter to chapter. She is my companion in the fire and my friend in the daylight. She only lives within my heart, but she is strong and steady. Always there when I need her. A loyal and compassionate beast. She was with me when I was a child. When I would hide in a closet somewhere to avoid the screaming. She was with me in the classroom, when I'd sink inside myself to avoid the constant shame of "not being good enough". She was with me as a teenager. When my insecurity manifested itself as addiction, self-inflicted pain, and rage. She was with me as a young adult. When I travelled to the West in search of a storm, with nothing but a car full of pots, pans, and a hopeful puppy. When I was desperately unsure of myself or the future. She is with me now. As a thirty-something-year-old who has experienced great triumphs and heartbreaks. Who has loved and lost. Who is still unsure of herself, but who is taking the time to learn and to grow. My horse. My beautiful, patient steed. She would writhe in my heart as I cried. She would dance in my soul when I conquered.

I do not take enough time to reach deep into my spirit and hug this guardian. I do not take enough trips into the desert of my mind with her. But I feel her. In everything I do, I feel her approaching gait and I can hear her playful neigh. I am sure, above all things that I am never left alone.

We will always want to steal a little bit of the light we're attracted to.

Look Up

Watch the clouds close in upon you
In a constant dance of blue and white.
As above, so below
For the sea dances the same dance.
Look up
Breathe in your present moment.
Carefully remember your place in the stars.
In a world where we are infinitely coerced into looking down
Or straight ahead,
Or into the future,
We should begin to ask what they don't want us to see.
And in complete and absolute defiance,
Look up.

I'm an amateur everything,
I've just never been afraid to start somewhere.

War of One

Night is the ship
That cradles me until morning
Holds me hostage while I sway
And wait for the sun

I ride on the backs
Of a fleet of a thousand horses
The bidding on my soul
Has surely begun

Restless from wandering
I empty my mind
And steady for the war
That is coming my way

A light descends
From a break in the sky
So I ready my heart
For a recognizable face

I feel my courage
Lessen with every second
Though this armor protects me
I'm wildly exposed

In this moment
I'm met with a shadowy reflection
I am stripped down
From my head to my toes

Although I am naked
I sense no danger
I feel a warmth of absolution
Wash through my blood

Hand to hand, heart to heart
I know this fair stranger
She is me; I am she
This has been a war of one.

Often, the best place to find ourselves
Is in the dark.

The Iron Horse

Quiet—
My eyes were not made for wandering
They lie,
Uneasy,
Searching for answers that have been lost for ages.

Crippling insecurities,
So much so,
I try to shake it
As my mother once did with the sheets and the
blankets.

Shake it until it's clean
Until I am safe to sleep

This town has changed.
Every lantern in every window
Has turned to grey.
Every tavern dweller has been replaced
Interchanged
With a new, silent, and weathered face.

I hear footsteps
Down the hall I was always afraid to stand in.
Every time I reach for the lights,
It's as if someone moved the switch.
When I opened by cowardly mouth,
It's as if someone changed the script.

This tired town
My tired hands
I thought I'd return a hero
But, still, no one knows who I am.

These buildings have aged
The patrons have too,
And the iron statue of a horse and cowboy
Signals this place is a safe refuge.

I can only stare
And hope that iron horse blinks
And stomps his frozen hooves
Telling me it's time we both ran,
As a knight and her horse do.

So I stare and I wish
But neither that iron horse,
Nor I,
Dare make a move.

Show me where I can find myself.
Take me to the sea, where two halves of my soul
may reunite.
Take me to the mountains, where I am reminded
that all hardships can be overcome.
Take me to the forest, where "as above, so below"
is my mantra.
Show me how to fall in love with my
surroundings,
And I will learn to fall in love,
With a thousand faces
And a million voices.

Fractures

Fractures
In every memory now

I can still see her reflection in the front door
Standing on the porch
Calling me for dinner

I'm too busy lying in the grass
Feeling the cold bristles in between my toes
Watching the planes fly low
Too busy creating dreams of myself commanding a shuttle
Headed towards the moon

To even notice her voice

Now, I wish I had absorbed every time she called for dinner
Or laughed in the kitchen for no apparent reason
A glass of wine in hand
Oldies playing on the radio
The sound of her sandals on the outdated tile floor
As she danced
With her sweetheart

They're fractured now,
These memories,
Sometimes they come across like an old home movie
Skipping;

Grey, frayed edges
Without a soundtrack or script
But I will never forget her bright blue eyes
Or the love for the life that she lived

Sometimes I still find myself
Lying in the grass
Cold bristles underneath my weathered feet
Watching the planes fly low
And I think
Maybe somewhere
She is looking down every once in awhile
To watch the planes below

Remembering how we laughed and cried
And took life with every aching curve
And although she visits me in my dreams,
What I wouldn't give to reach out and hold her

But alas—
Only memories I'm left with,
Only these tiny little fractures.

Note to Self:

So many nice things.
Nice house.
Nice car.
Nice job.
I'm grateful for all of it, but none of it makes me happy.
It scares me.
It all feels fragile and conditional.
I can only keep the nice things if I play by the rules.
Comfort is a veil, shielding my soul from tapping into
something bigger.
Luxury is the lie that keeps me from diving into the
unknown.
I've built beautiful walls around me.
Decorated with fine art and fresh paint.
Only to divide myself from the real world—
I've made myself such a pretty little cage.
When I look at these things, I don't feel safe or loved,
I feel conned by myself.
I feel anxious and immature.
So here I sit in a cold and lifeless house,
Windows between me and the birds
Wood panels between me and the trees.
Do you think they see me hiding?
Do they see me peering from the edges of their old friends or enemies?

Will I sell it all and live as a naked vagabond running
aimlessly through the woods?
Can I quit my job?
Can I toss the cards and flip the table?
I no longer wish to play.

But I light the candle I light every morning,
I shower a hot and privileged shower,
I sit at my desk and I turn on the laptop.
Sip my coffee and glance longingly out the window—
At the birds and the trees.
I wish it was easier to step off the theater stage.
But maybe it's not so bad here, after all . . .
Maybe I rather enjoy my little cage.

Spiders

There's a spider on my wall today.
A thistly little thing with her legs sprawled across my
favorite poster
Reaching for the edges
Like her, I've weaved a tired web around myself
She begs for food
I beg for words
We're not so different, her and I
Normally, I would capture her in an old mason jar
And put her in the grass
Today I watch her
I study her
Why am I so afraid of you, tiny one?
Why do I feel you racing down my back and biting at
my sides?
Such a harmless, valiant widow
As am I

On Death

I often wonder if I'd ever missed a path
Specifically carved for my feet.
A path desperately waiting to be tread
But a path left undiscovered.
Did I ever overlook, or blatantly ignore,
Something critical to my story?
Did I turn over, erase, re-write or burn the pages of
what could have been a beautiful novel?
Is there such a thing?
Is there ever more than one path?
Am I cursed with free will?
Or plagued with pre-destination?
Other times I feel like the edge of the horizon is where
the projections cease—
All that truly exists is whatever I can see.
Tell me
Do you really think you would live differently
If you knew you were going to die tomorrow?
Would I learn to paint and move to Bali?
Meditate in Tibet and jump out of airplanes?
I always feel like I'm going to die tomorrow
And yet
I drink and I mope
I do the dishes and I sit on the couch
All to distract myself from the fact
That I am, indeed, dying.
And so are you.
I still don't know how to paint.
I've never been to Bali or Tibet.

I'm bad at meditating and I hate flying.
Maybe the only thing that makes me feel truly alive is
remembering
There is a one hundred percent certainty
That I will die.
I'm grateful, I suppose.
Death, however mysterious,
Is very well the only sure thing in this human experience.

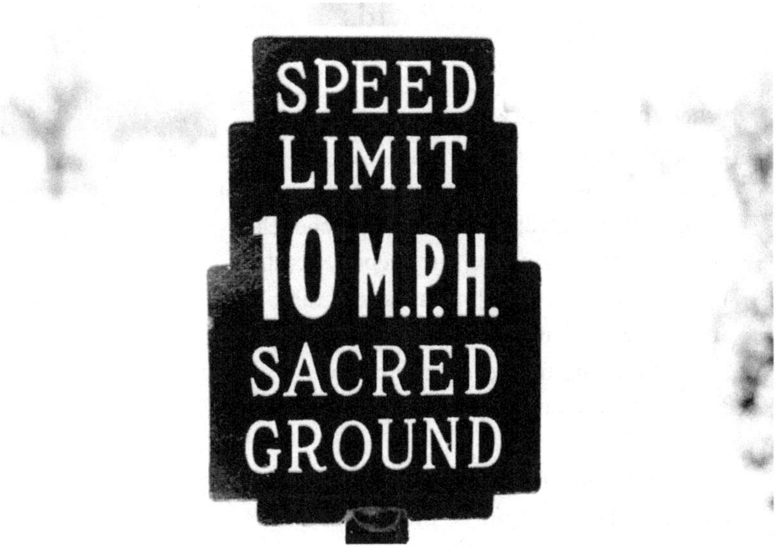
SPEED
LIMIT
10 M.P.H.
SACRED
GROUND

Kids

What unkempt kids we are
Banging on pots and pans
Or anything we can get our sticky little hands on
Lying in the grass after a fistful of psychedelics,
Feet in the air discussing our deepest secrets
Watching our surroundings twist and turn
Sometimes we laugh, sometimes we cry
Some moments are meant to reminisce
And others are meant for brand new creations

I've wanted this tribe for so long
I looked for meaningful connection in all the wrong places.
I find myself full of childlike awe
As I observe the freedom in these people—
Wild
Absolutely wild beings full of empathy, passion, hurt
and drive
The perfect recipe for greatness
The soup of kindred souls
My hands are placed on the beating heart of this group
I can feel it's pulse in my veins
We are one here
I look around at what we've made
I soak it in and humbly accept my role
I brave up, I bow down

There's no room for judgment here
There can only be grace
And in the midst of it all,

At the crux of our youth,
Although we may want to conquer the world;
Ultimately,
What we're yearning for
Is to love and be loved.

Babylon

Boom.
Here we are.
That moment when we part ways.
That place we always promised we'd never be.
We've proven that the harder you love someone,
The harder they become your enemy.
Every secret.
Every fetish.
Every kiss stolen in the dark,
Suddenly are ammunition in a war that neither of us wanted to
start.
Every promise.
Every commitment.
Now just reasons not to trust.
Who can promise forever?
I can't blame you for tapping out.
I can't blame myself any more than I already have.
Got us a great, big king-sized bed
Just so we could sleep farther apart from each other.
Love is not a promise, I guess.
Love is not a word.
It's a painstaking daily allegiance.
I was never meant to be your loyal patriot.
I wear so many uniforms,
I fall in love with every nation.
Although, at one point,
You were my favorite.
No matter where we were,
We spoke the same language.

In came Babylon.
We built higher and higher,
But we never built a sturdy home.
On our quest to build a castle to Heaven,
We ended up isolated and alone.
And in one swift motion from god, our whoever,
Our tethered language broke.
Those waves of wrath separated our fates
And every brick we laid to solidify our faith in each other
Finally crumbled.
Who knew we were building a paper castle?
Who knew that our love was so fragile?

Walls aren't meant to keep us safe,
They're meant to keep us in

I've neared a place in this book where I'm not sure I have anything of use to say. Maybe this is the part they call "the end". I've heard of it before. I didn't ever think I'd see it with my own eyes. I assumed it was a mythical creature that only devout believers and mystics could conjure. Yet, here I am. End. A beautiful and complicated location.

I've always used writing to expel my own demons. I'm not a novelist. I'm not a storyteller. I'm a me-teller. The only thing I can do is write with a blazing and honest fury in hopes that someone else might be able to interpret the code. Writing is a fortress. It's a place where I can surround myself with invisible pages and sink deep into a trance of my own choosing. It's the most controllable high I've ever known.

With every high, however, comes a point of impenetrable and debilitating doubt. There's a crossroad at every altered reality where you feel yourself suck abruptly back into your body to ask, "is it real"? Am I really experiencing a life-altering journey or am I standing nose-to-wall, drooling down my chin, and mumbling indistinctly? Maybe both can exist simultaneously and perhaps I am a bit of all these things. A me-teller, a mumbler, and an addict.

This book has been an unrestrained ride. I took the seatbelt off a long time ago and let the emotions take a hold of the keys. There was no reason to hold back here. There was no one to impress and there was certainly no face to save. I just wanted a space to say . . . whatever the hell I felt like saying. I don't feel any more a writer now than I did four months ago when I swore to see this project through. I do, however, feel that I have things to say. A drooling mumbling drunk of a poet? Perhaps. There is always that off chance, though, that I am someone's sorceress, stoking a flame in some stranger's heart. There is a gamble that this could be kindling, just one small branch, for a much bigger fire.

One More Thing

There will always need to be a little bit more. Don't you love the taste of iron? That warm rush of liquid metal on your tongue when you've nervously chomped away at the inside of your cheek? That is life, coursing through you.

There will always need to be a little bit more. You've finished a book. You've recorded an album. You've learned how to fly a goddamn jet. You've joined the Peace Corps, you've forgiven your mother, you've had a child.

There will always need to be a little bit more. Happiness is not found on a signature line below the fine print. Fulfillment is not a car on the lot you can open the doors, check the tire pressure, and speed down the road to test for safety. It has no price tag. No tangibility.

There will always need to be a little bit more. The moment you get that job, the second you sell out the stadium, the first book signing, the last time you ever have to deliver a pizza to pay rent. It won't be enough to fill the void. You, artist, can never stop. Stopping is not an option. "Stop" is not a word in your dictionary. There is only "what's next"? You are not entitled to greatness or mastery. It is a lifestyle. It is intentional.

When you lie awake in bed at night and can't sleep because you know that every single second you're not using your hands and mind to create something new is a wasted second; that's when you know. That is your poking and prying need to be constantly alert. Tap into your passion, creator, and lean so far into it that you will lose your fear of falling. You are called to get out of that bed and make use of those hands. Everything you do and everything you make has a deeper ripple than you could ever fathom. So, close the chapter, pat yourself on the back, celebrate your success and revel in it for a moment. And then? Get back to it.

There will always need to be a little bit more.

Made in the USA
Middletown, DE
16 August 2022

71173673R00046